Be Your Best...

Eating Fruits and Vegetables

A to Z

by Catherine Anderson-Barnes

Copyrighted Material

Be Your Best...Eating Fruits and Vegetables A to Z

ISBN: 979-8-9873416-1-2

Library of Congress Control Number: 1-11941554471

Cover Design and Book Layout Provided by Brock Merritt
Inside Cover and Interior Design by Elena Shelest
Illustrations Provided by ElenaArtBy, MUJKA, and AMB illustrations

First Printed in the United States

For more information contact
Instagram @catherineandersonbarnes
or caabarnes2@gmail.com

CAB

www.catherineandersonbarnes.com

ABOUT THE AUTHOR:

Catherine Anderson-Barnes
has over 25 years of experience as a health and nutrition educator. She has instructed all age groups; however, her love and passion is with educating young children.

"Be Your Best...Eating Fruits and Vegetables A to Z"
was written to give children an opportunity to learn the important role fruits and vegetables play in a healthy body.

This bright-colored book is comprised of a collection of delightfully charming fruits, vegetables, and children. The array of vivid colors shown in the fruits and vegetables are much like the beautiful colors in the rainbow and should serve as a great reminder for us to choose a variety of rainbow-colored fruits and vegetables for optimal health.

It is Catherine's desire that your child will be mesmerized by the whimsical fruit and vegetables, be captivated by the beautiful and diverse children, and be entertained identifying which body parts benefit from consuming colorful fruits and vegetables.

She also hopes that you will encourage your child to try new fruits and vegetables, and be patient as you do. It can take many tries before your child will try and/or like new foods. Some fruits and vegetables may look unusual. Be an inspiration to your child by eating your fruits and vegetables and inspire them to discover beauty in everything – you just need to look for the good and positive in everything and everybody.

"Be Your Best"
every day...
"From Your Head Down To Your Feet."

Graphics and Illustrations

Elena Shelest – ElenaArtBy
MUJKA – mujkadesign
AMBillustrations
AquarelleSpace
Brock Merritt

In
Honor
Of
C.P.
♥
Love
You
Always
C.C.

Aa

Apple

Be Your Best From Head To Feet...
Fruits And Vegetables Are A Must To Eat!

Eating apples help to keep these body parts healthy!

Bb

Banana

Be Your Best From Head To Feet...
Fruits And Vegetables Are A Must To Eat!

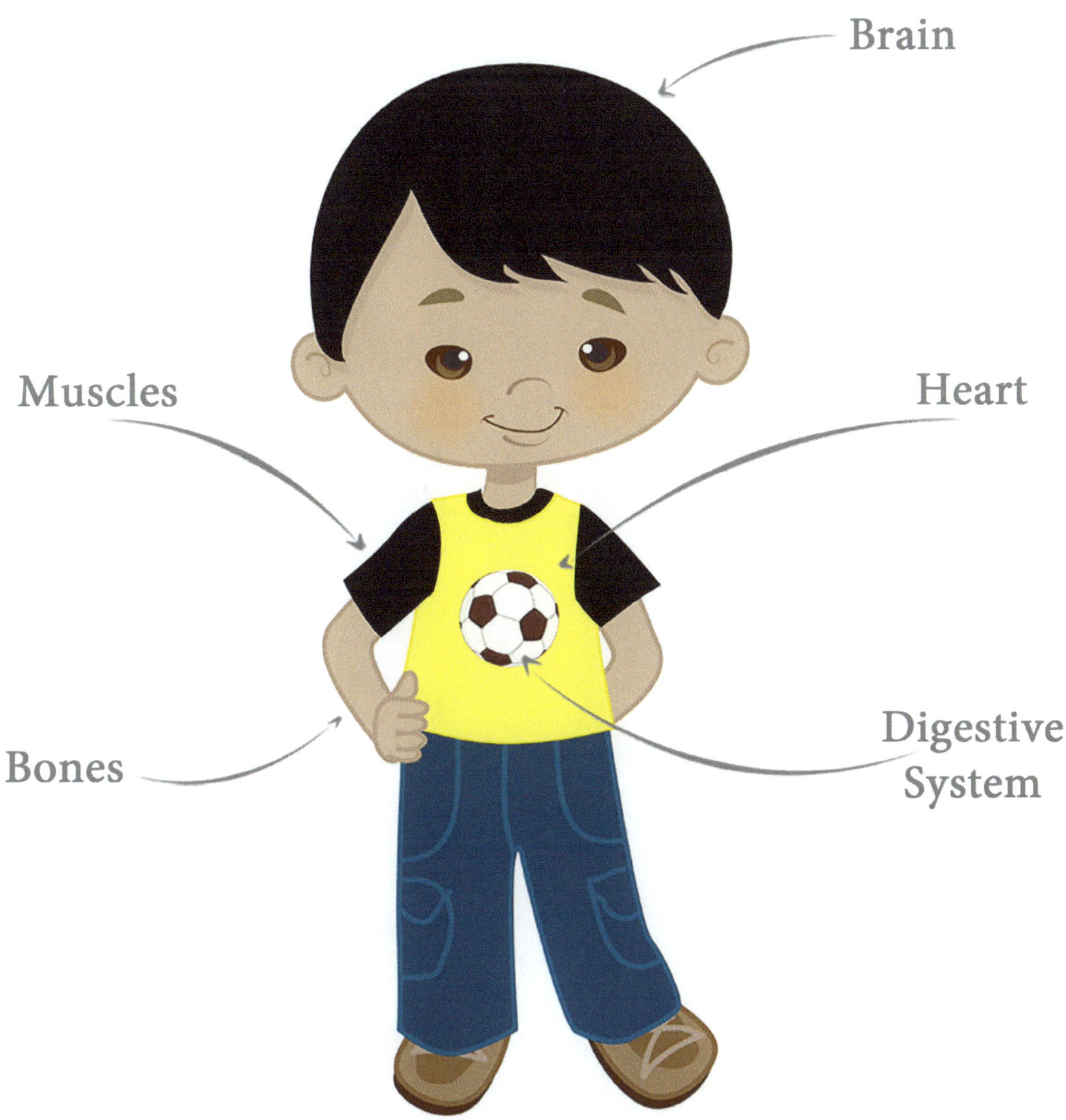

Eating bananas help to keep these body parts healthy!

Cc

Carrot

Be Your Best From Head To Feet... Fruits And Vegetables Are A Must To Eat!

Eating carrots help to keep these body parts healthy!

Dd

Dragon Fruit

Be Your Best From Head To Feet...
Fruits And Vegetables Are A Must To Eat!

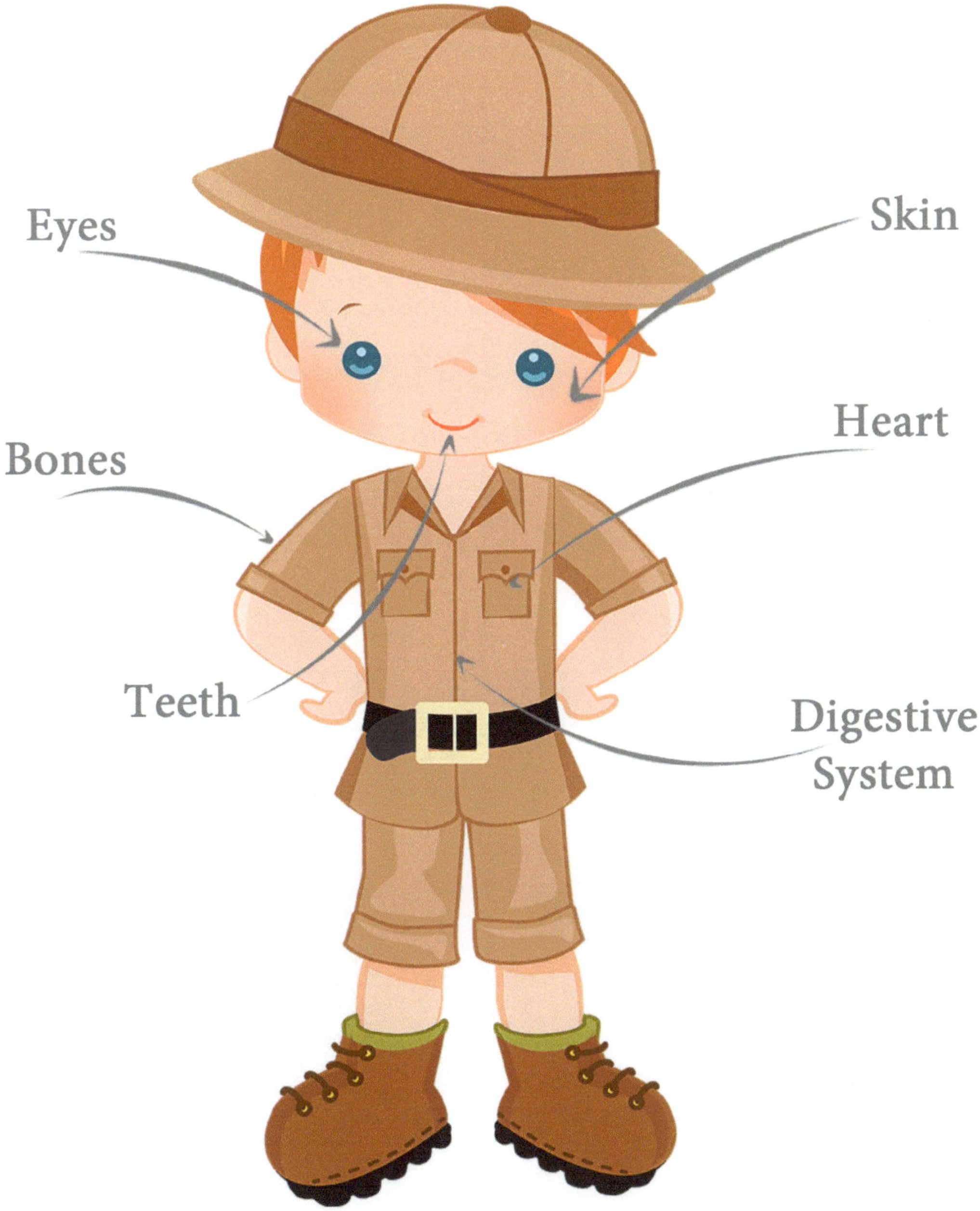

Eating dragon fruit helps to keep these body parts healthy!

Ee

Eggplant

Be Your Best From Head To Feet...
Fruits And Vegetables Are A Must To Eat!

Eating eggplant helps to keep these body parts healthy!

Ff

Fig

Be Your Best From Head To Feet... Fruits And Vegetables Are A Must To Eat!

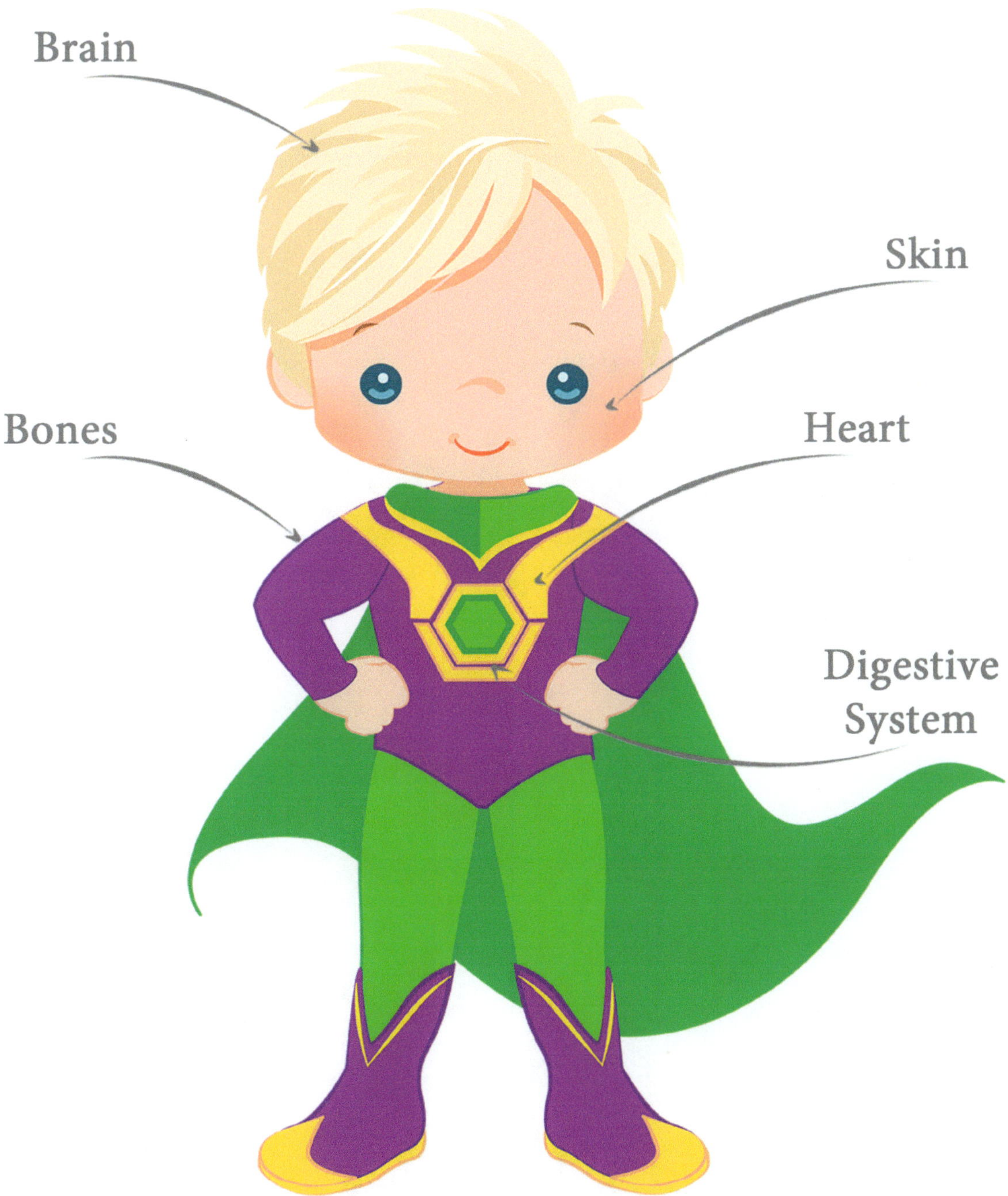

Eating figs help to keep these body parts healthy!

Gg

Grapefruit

Be Your Best From Head To Feet...
Fruits And Vegetables Are A Must To Eat!

Eating grapefruit helps to keep these body parts healthy!

Hh

Honeydew Melon

Be Your Best From Head To Feet...
Fruits And Vegetables Are A Must To Eat!

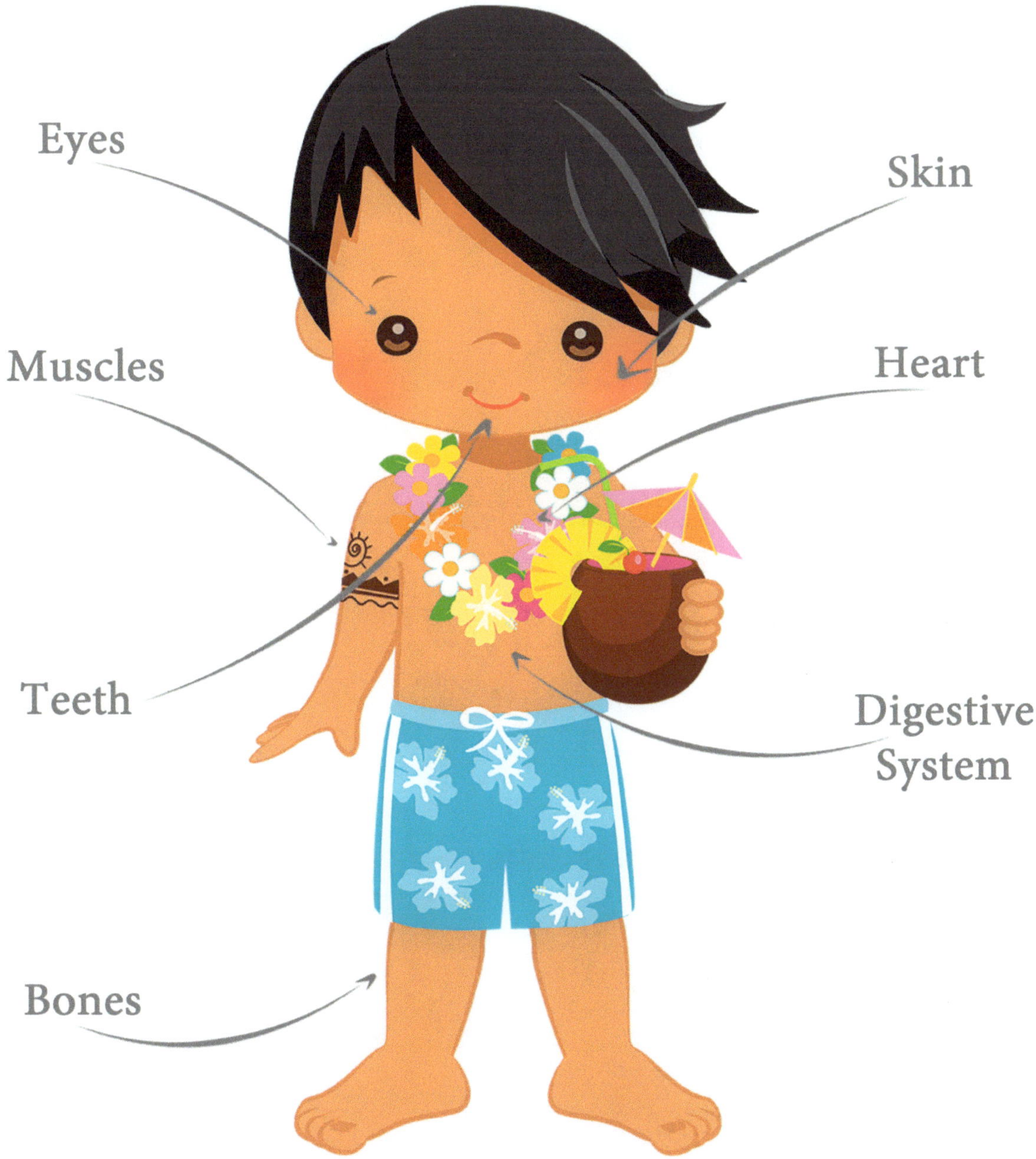

Eating honeydew melon helps to keep these body parts healthy!

Ii

Iceberg Lettuce

Be Your Best From Head To Feet...
Fruits And Vegetables Are A Must To Eat!

Eating iceberg lettuce helps to keep these body parts healthy!

Jj

Jackfruit

Be Your Best From Head To Feet... Fruits And Vegetables Are A Must To Eat!

Eating jackfruit helps to keep these body parts healthy!

Kk

Kiwi Fruit

Be Your Best From Head To Feet... Fruits And Vegetables Are A Must To Eat!

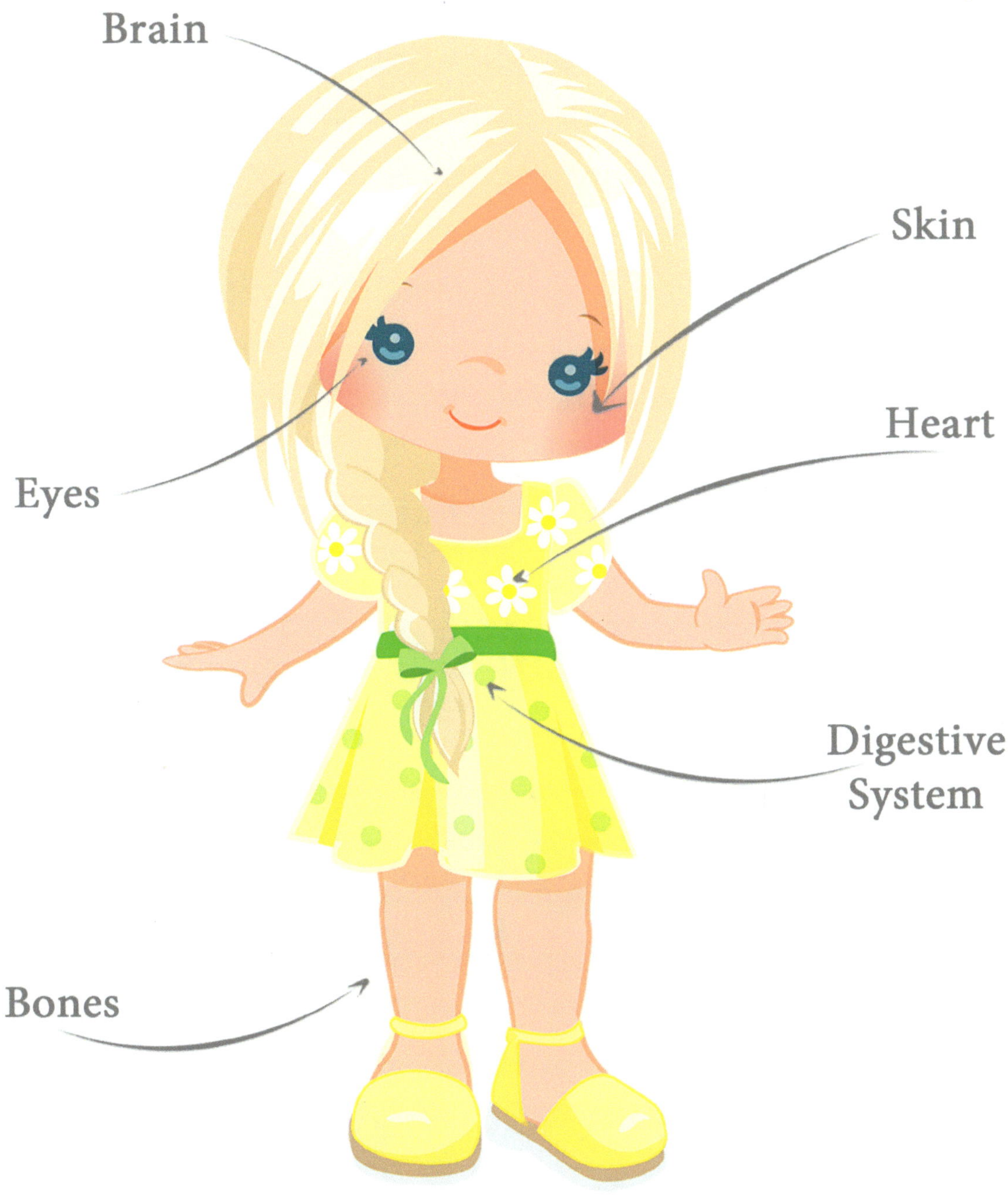

Eating kiwi fruit helps to keep these body parts healthy!

Ll

Lemon

Be Your Best From Head To Feet... Fruits And Vegetables Are A Must To Eat!

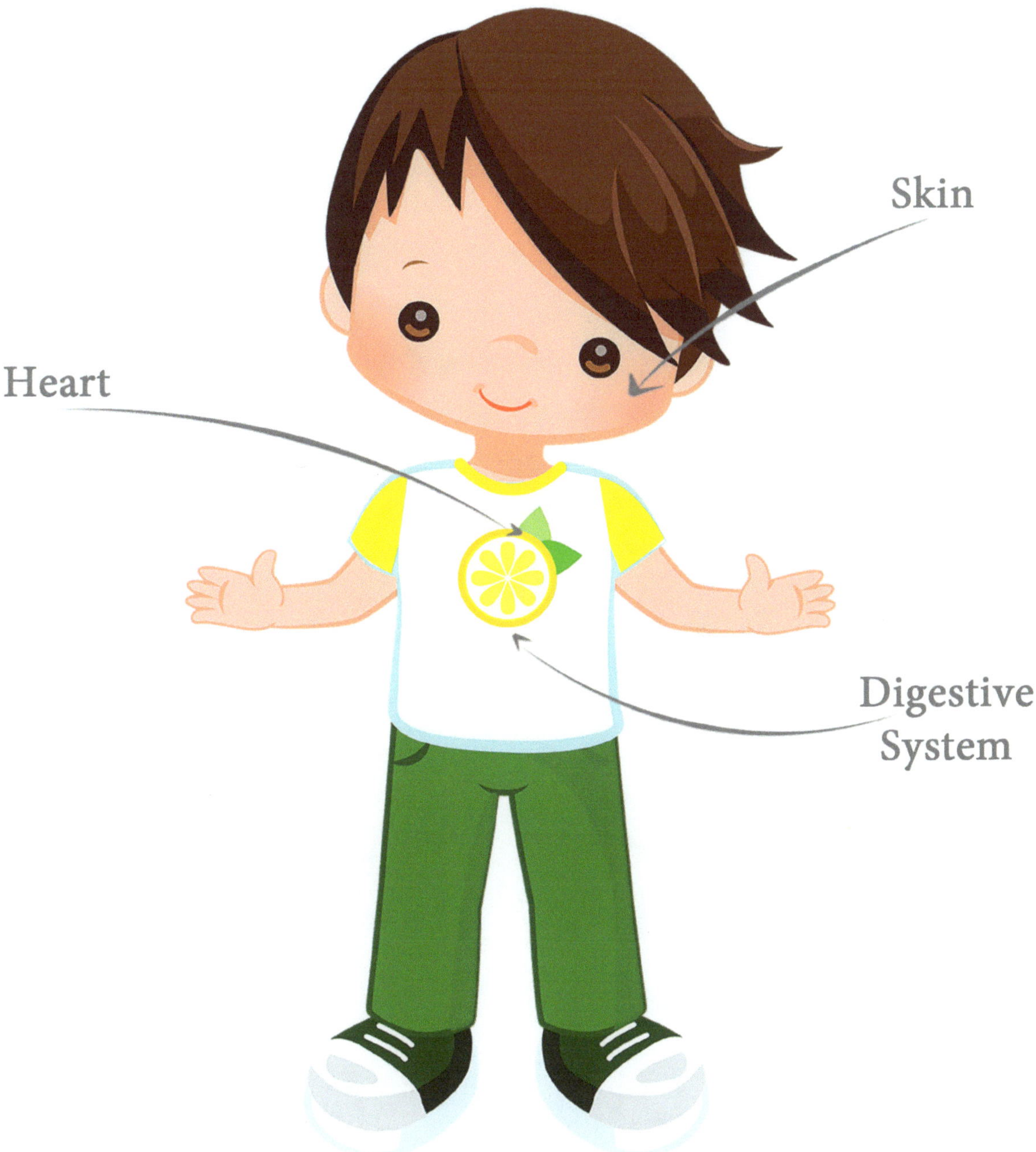

Eating lemons help to keep these body parts healthy!

Mm

Mango

Be Your Best From Head To Feet...
Fruits And Vegetables Are A Must To Eat!

Eating mangos help to keep these body parts healthy!

Nn

Nectarine

Be Your Best From Head To Feet...
Fruits And Vegetables Are A Must To Eat!

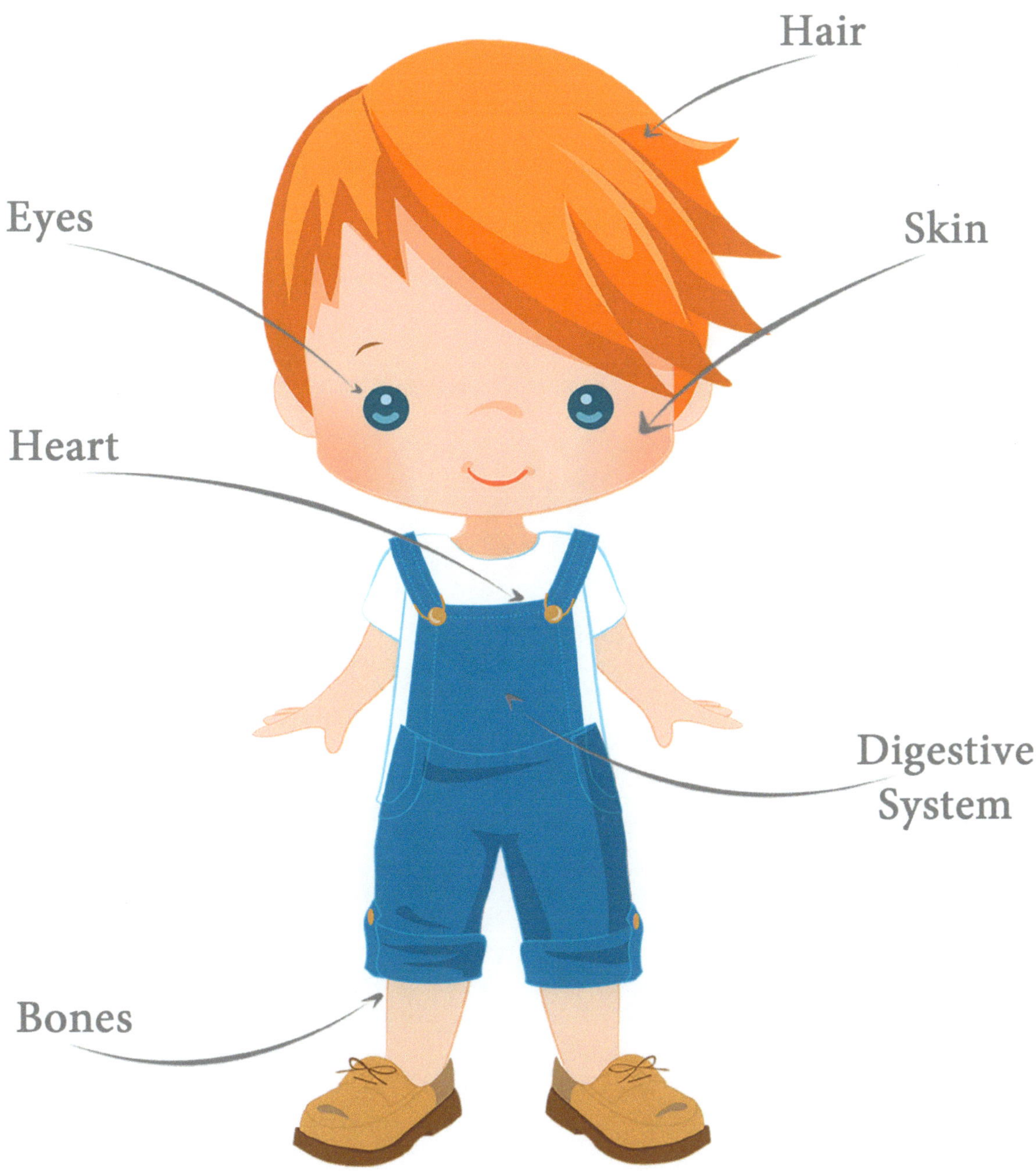

Eating nectarines help to keep these body parts healthy!

Oo

Orange

Be Your Best From Head To Feet... Fruits And Vegetables Are A Must To Eat!

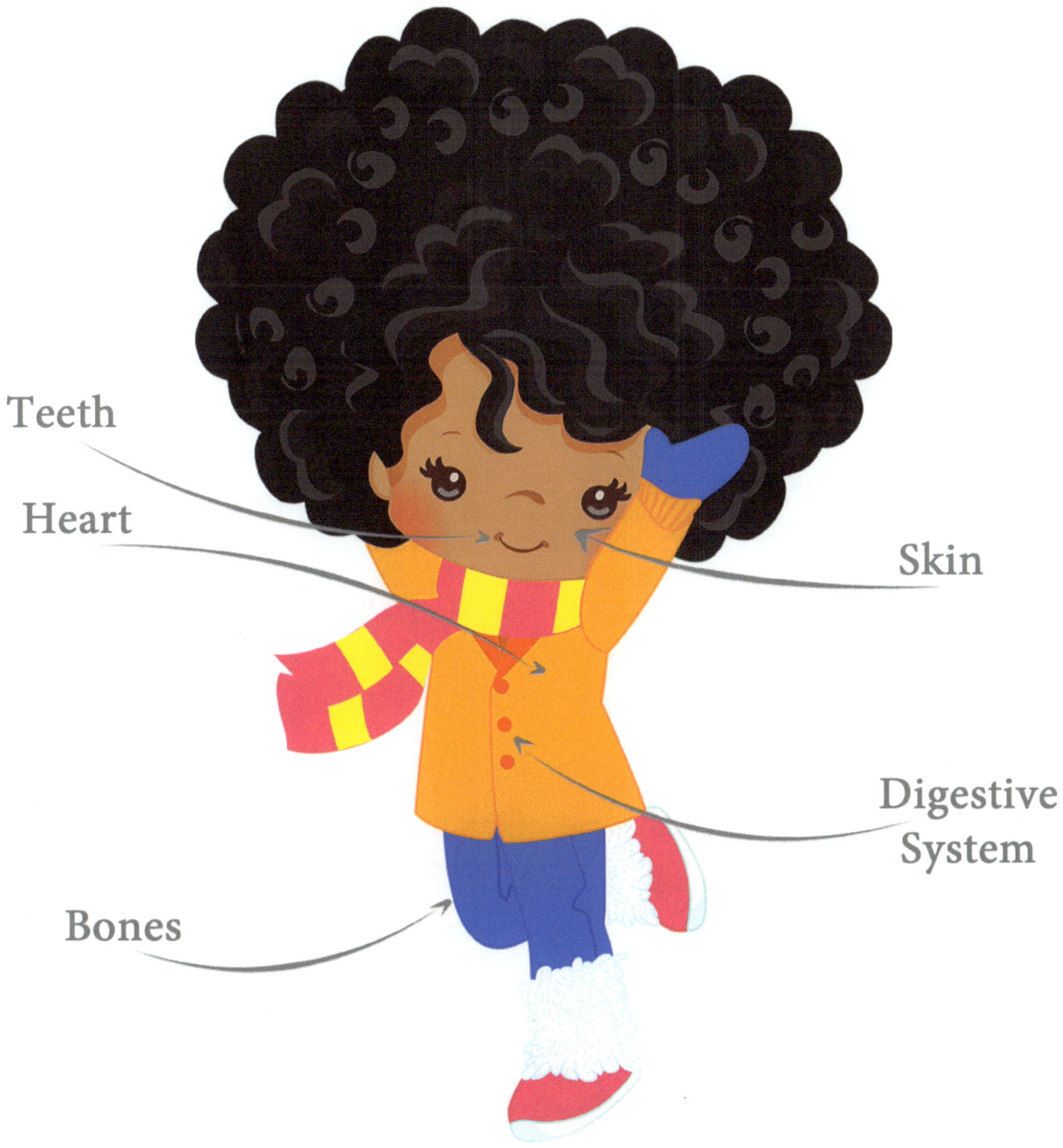

Eating oranges help to keep these body parts healthy!

Pp

Pumpkin

Be Your Best From Head To Feet... Fruits And Vegetables Are A Must To Eat!

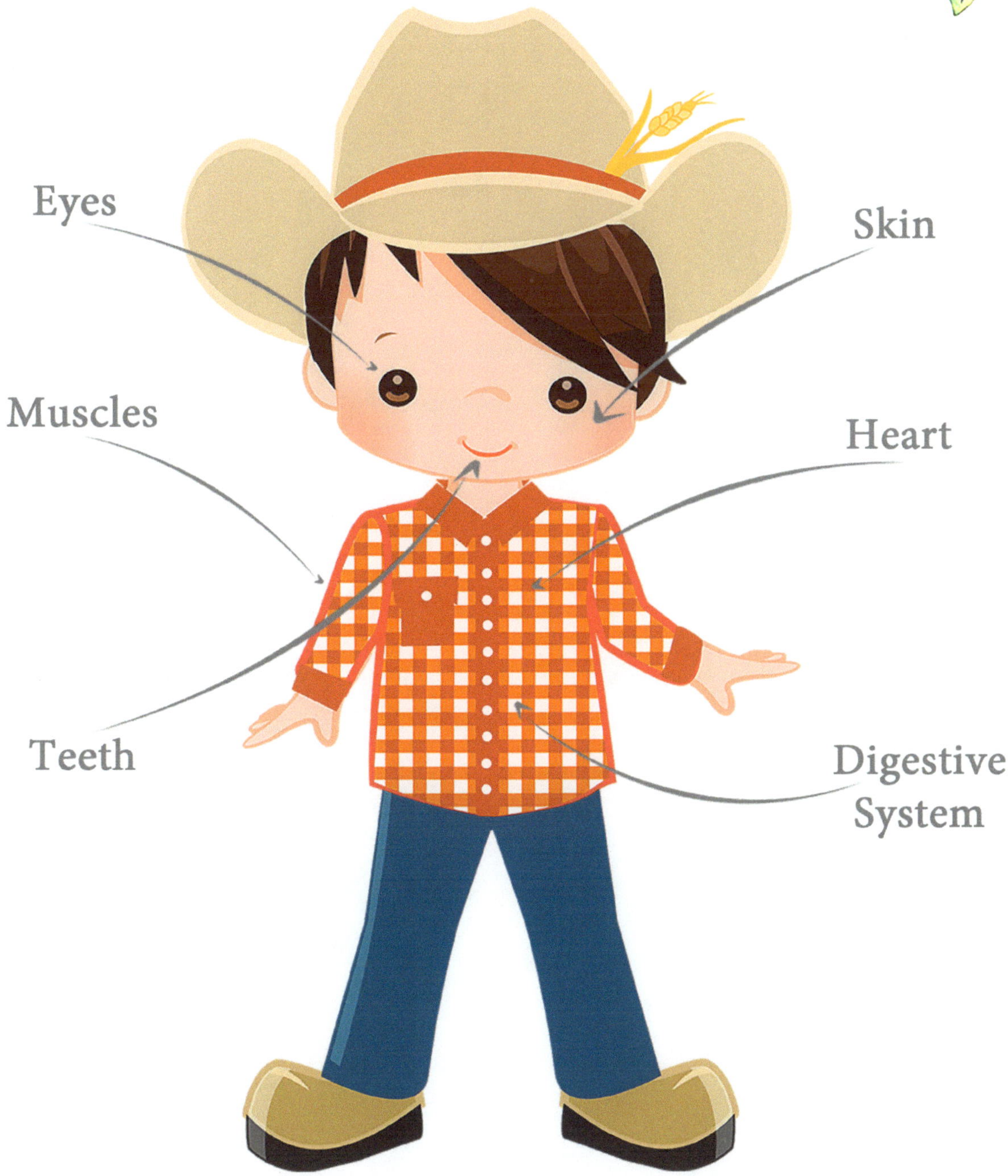

Eating pumpkin helps to keep these body parts healthy!

Qq

Quince

Be Your Best From Head To Feet... Fruits And Vegetables Are A Must To Eat!

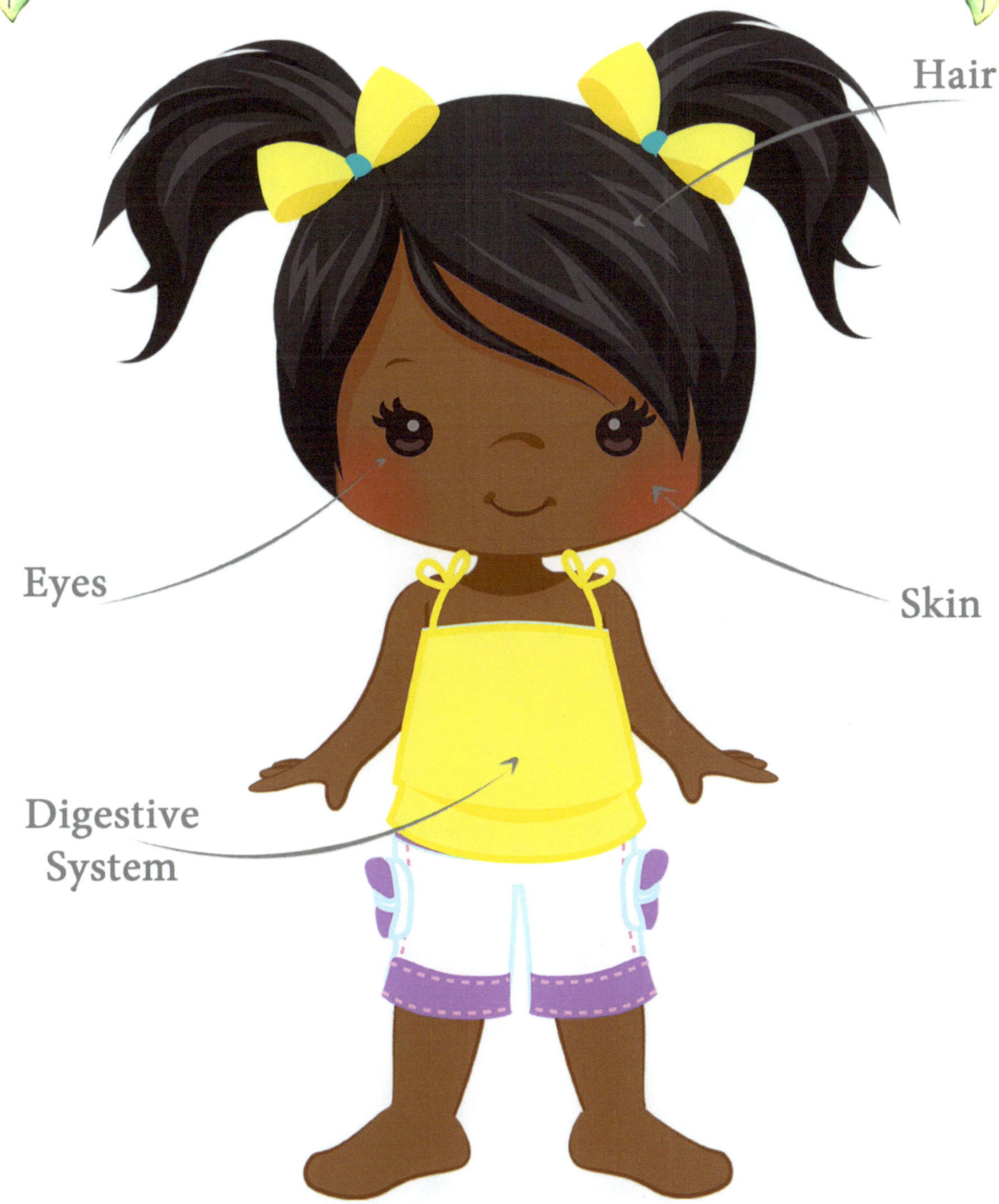

Eating quince helps to keep these body parts healthy!

Rr

Raspberries

Be Your Best From Head To Feet... Fruits And Vegetables Are A Must To Eat!

Eating raspberries help to keep these body parts healthy!

Ss

Strawberries

Be Your Best From Head To Feet...
Fruits And Vegetables Are A Must To Eat!

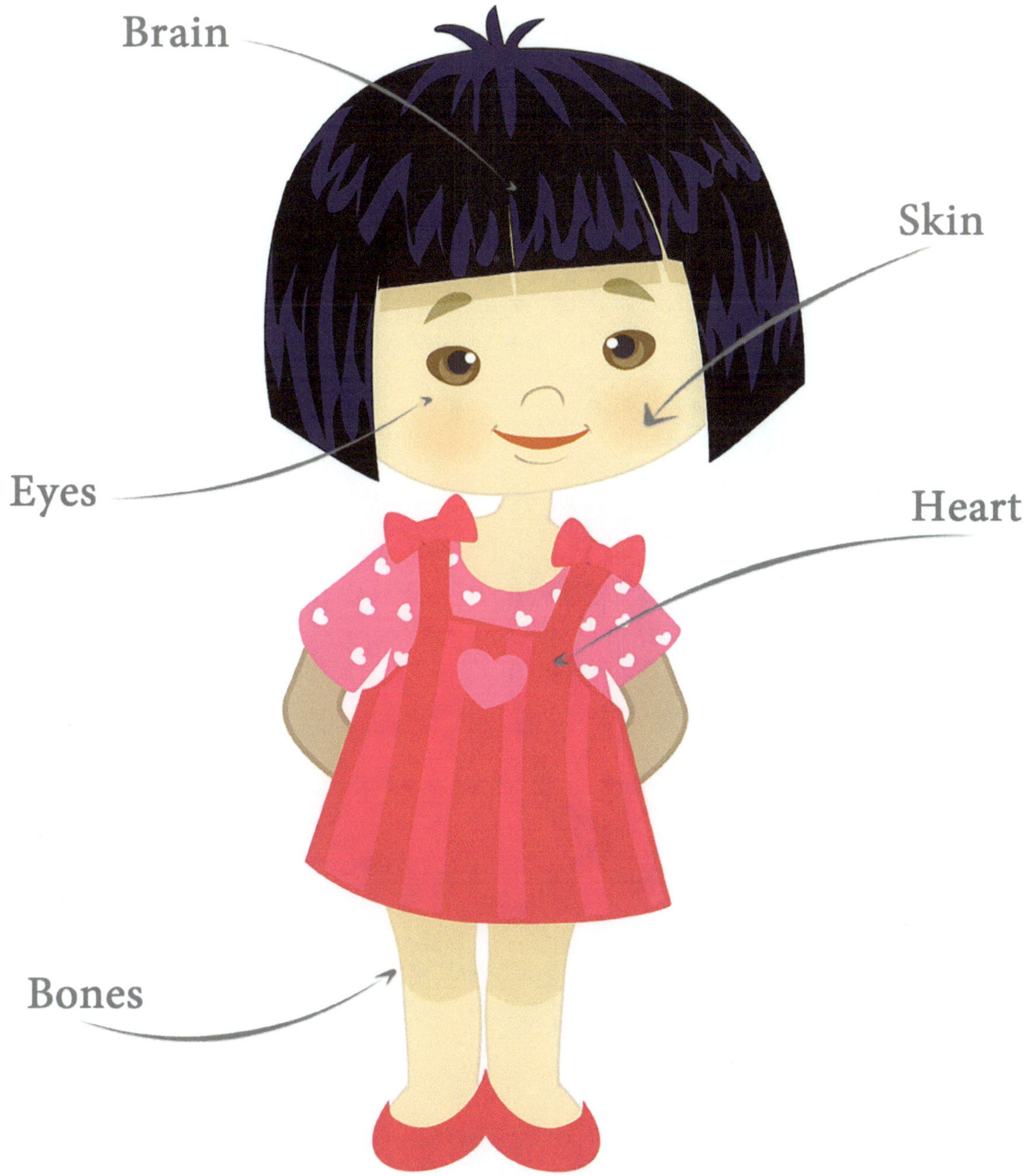

Eating strawberries help to keep these body parts healthy!

Tt

Tomatoes

Be Your Best From Head To Feet... Fruits And Vegetables Are A Must To Eat!

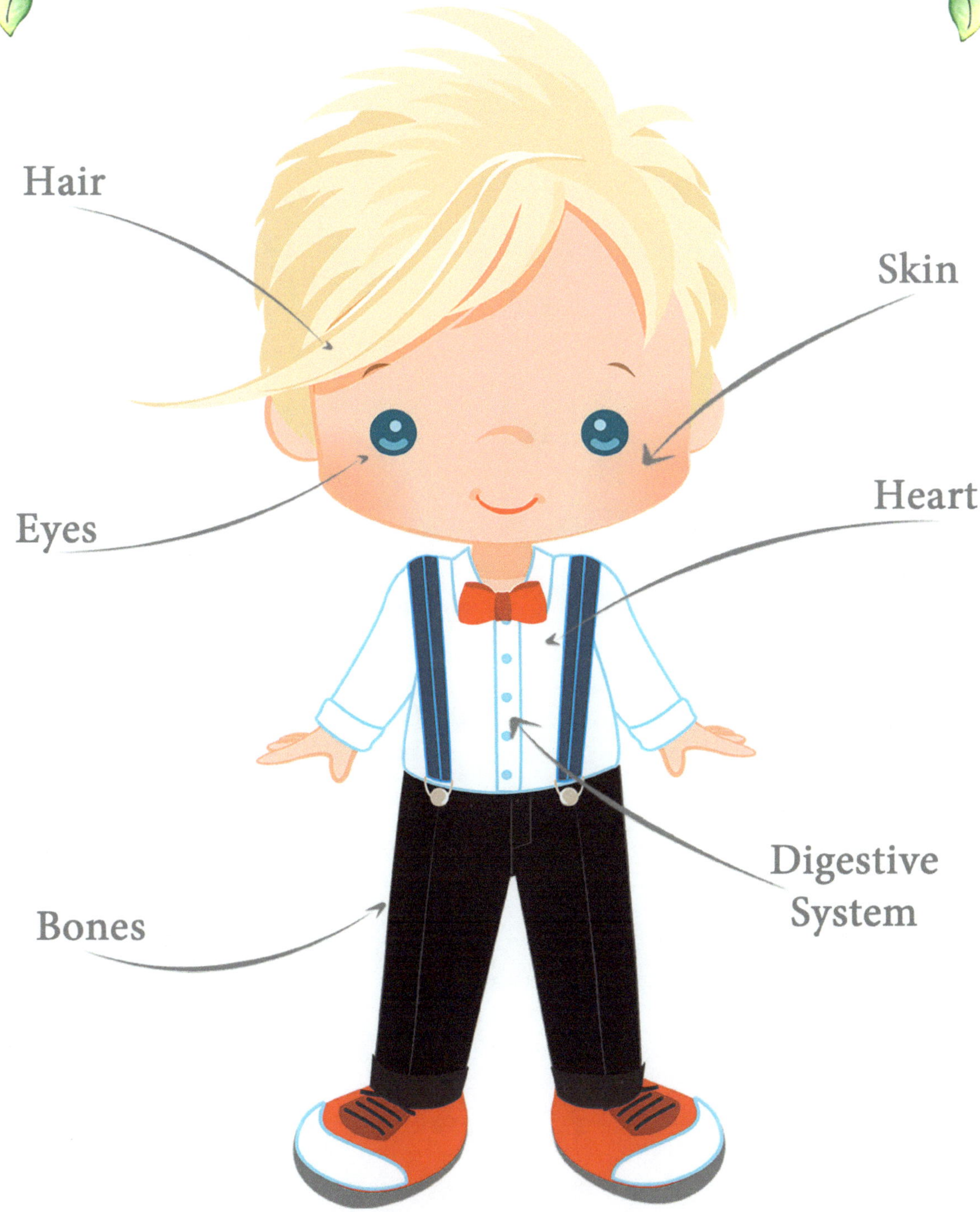

Eating tomatoes help to keep these body parts healthy!

Uu

Uglifruit

Be Your Best From Head To Feet...
Fruits And Vegetables Are A Must To Eat!

Eating uglifruit helps to keep these body parts healthy!

Vv

Vidalia Onion

**Be Your Best From Head To Feet...
Fruits And Vegetables Are A Must To Eat!**

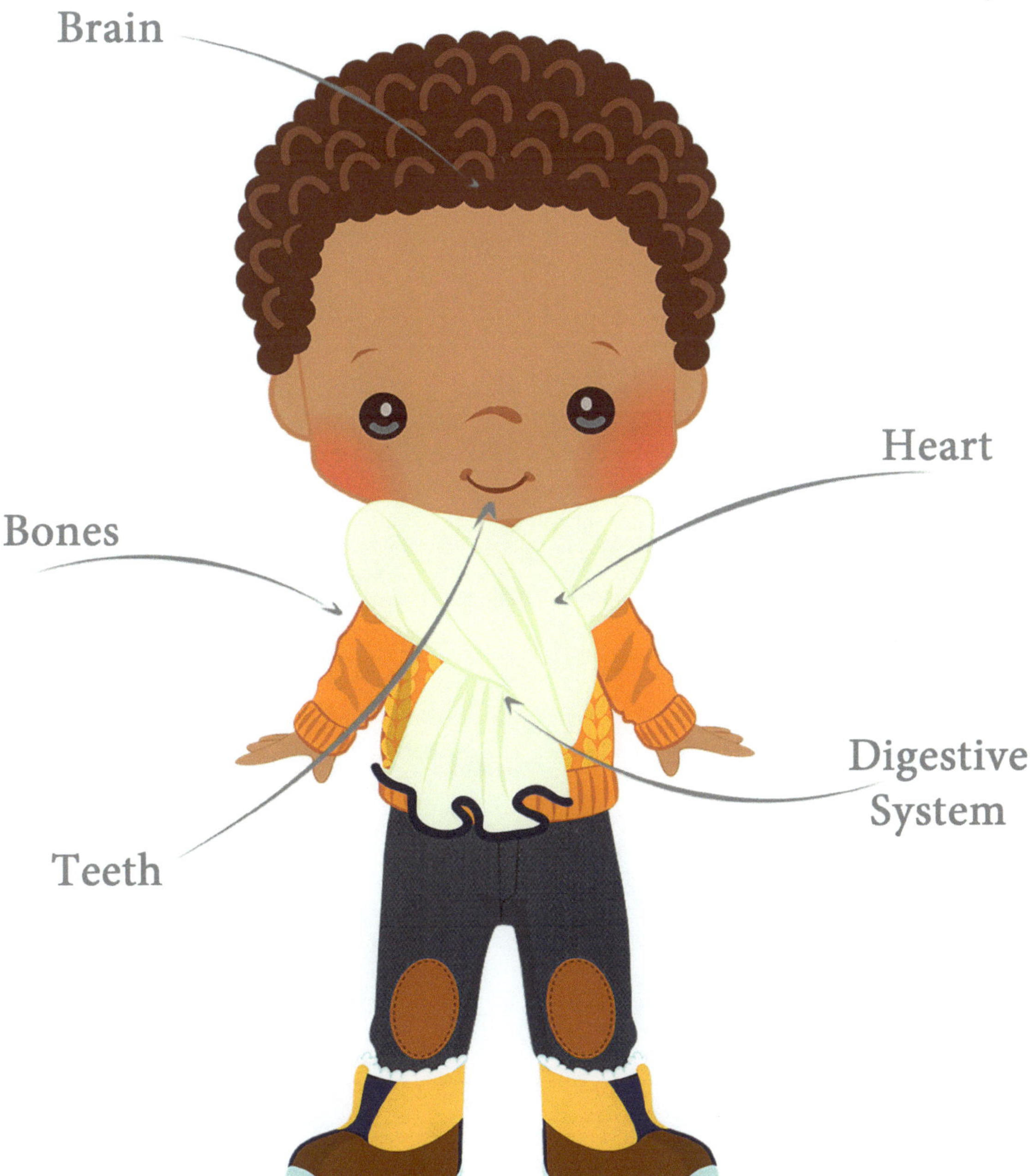

Eating vidalia onions help to keep these body parts healthy!

Ww

Watermelon

Be Your Best From Head To Feet... Fruits And Vegetables Are A Must To Eat!

Eating watermelon helps to keep these body parts healthy!

Xx

Xinomavro Grapes

Be Your Best From Head To Feet...
Fruits And Vegetables Are A Must To Eat!

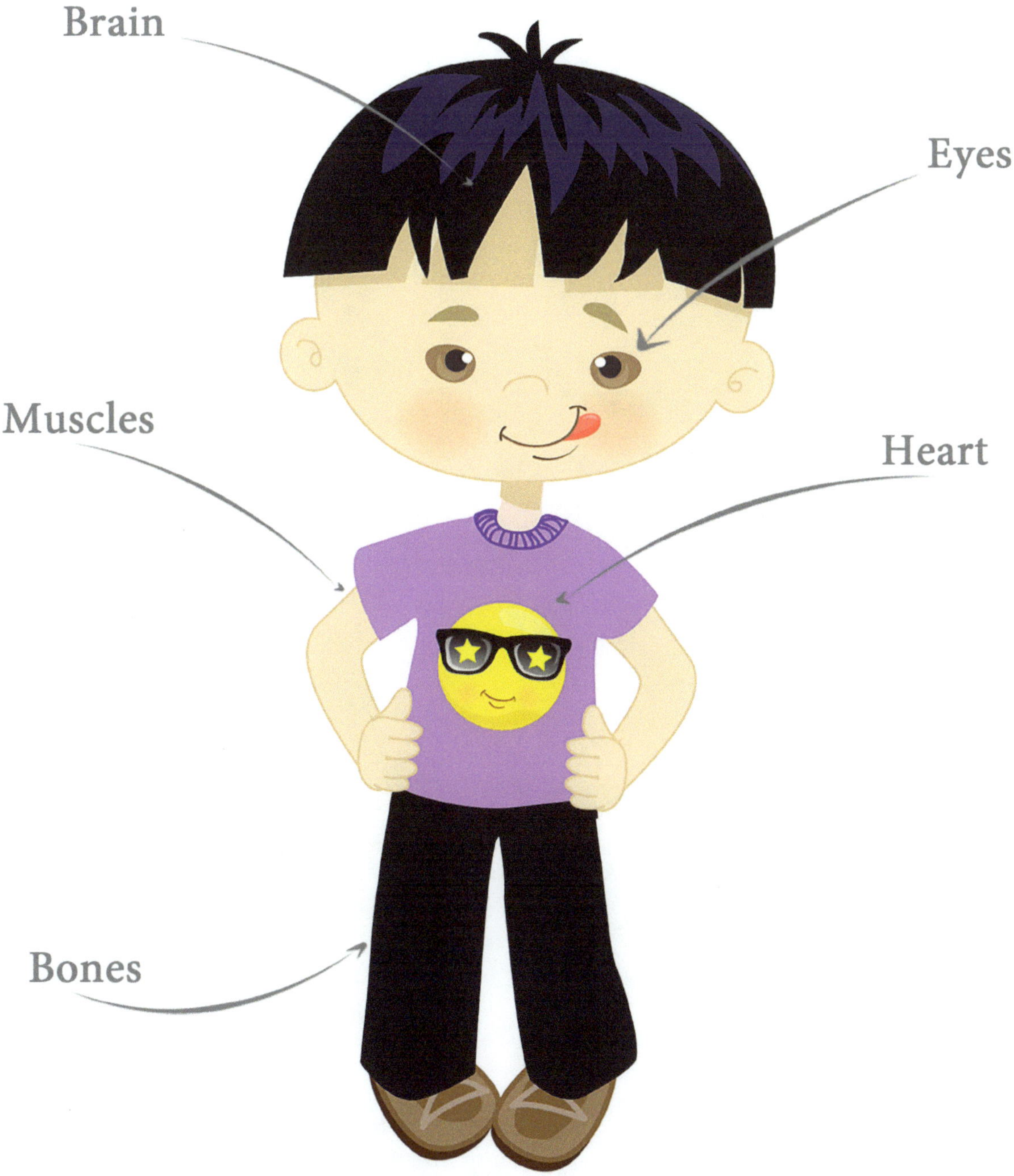

Eating xinomavro grapes help to keep these body parts healthy!

Yy

Yellow Pepper

Be Your Best From Head To Feet... Fruits And Vegetables Are A Must To Eat!

Eating yellow peppers help to keep these body parts healthy!

Zz

Zucchini

Be Your Best From Head To Feet...
Fruits And Vegetables Are A Must To Eat!

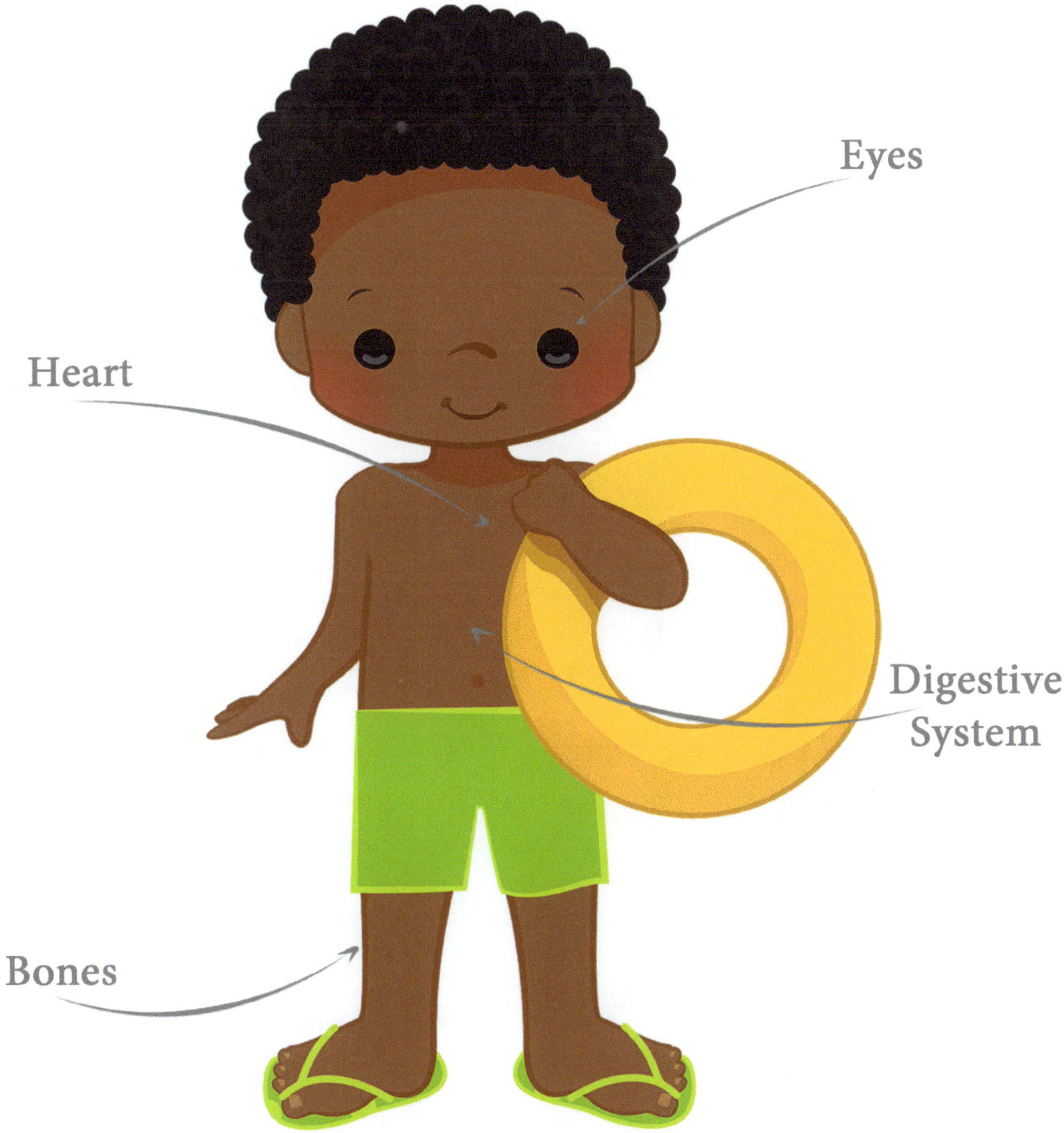

Eating zucchini helps to keep these body parts healthy!

The

End

Parent Piece

How Much Fruits and Vegetables Do Children Need Daily?

Girls

Age	Fruits	Vegetables
2-3	1 cup	1 cup
4-8	1-1½ cups	1½ cups
9-13	1½ cups	2 cups
14-18	1½ cups	2½ cups

Boys

Age	Fruits	Vegetables
2-3	1 cup	1 cup
4-8	1-1½ cups	1½ cups
9-13	1½ cups	2½ cups
14-18	2 cups	3 cups

SOURCE:USDA, www.ChooseMyPlate.gov

Helping Children to Eat Fruits and Vegetables

Fruits and vegetables are particularly significant for the good health of children. By helping your children develop healthy eating habits now, you will be protecting them later in life. Vitamins, minerals, fiber, and protective substances called phytochemicals found in the different colored types of fruits and vegetables help children grow and develop properly. They also help your family maintain cardiovascular health, keep body weight under control, prevent birth defects, lower cancer risks, and live longer, healthier, more productive lives. Teaching children to eat for optimal health is a tremendous gift that will have lifelong benefits.

EATING A RAINBOW

Eating five servings of fruits and vegetables a day is extremely important. By eating fruits and vegetables of a variety of different colors, one can get the best all-around health benefits. Each different color fruit and vegetable is comprised of unique health components that are vital to our health. Therefore, strive to make half your plate comprised of fruits and vegetables and be assured you are consuming these vitally essential nutrients!

RED fruits and vegetables contain the phytochemicals lycopene and anthocyanins that help maintain a healthy heart, urinary tract health, memory function, and lower the risk of some cancers.

YELLOW/ORANGE fruits and vegetables contain antioxidants like vitamin C and phytochemicals like carotenoids and bioflavonoids that help maintain a healthy immune system, heart, vision health, and lower the risk of some cancers.

GREEN fruits and vegetables contain the phytochemicals lutein and indoles that maintain vision health, promotes strong teeth and bones, and lower the risk of some cancers.

PURPLE/BLUE fruits and vegetables contain health-promoting phytochemicals such as anthocyanins and phenolics that are currently being studied for their antioxidant and anti-aging benefits. Including purple and blue fruits and vegetables in your diet will help maintain urinary tract health, memory function, healthy aging, and lower the risk of some cancers.

WHITE/TAN/BROWN fruits and vegetables contain phytochemicals like allicin and selenium that help to maintain a hearty heart, healthy cholesterol levels, and lower the risk of some cancers.

ADAPTED FROM:
Blythedale Children's Hospital *Eat Well, Be Well* nutrition outreach program

Tips for Getting Children to Eat Fruits and Vegetables

MAKE IT EASY AND ACCESSIBLE: Children reach for convenient snacks when they are hungry. Place washed fruits in a bowl on the table and washed and cut fruits and vegetables at their eye level in the refrigerator.

MAKE IT INTERESTING: Children often prefer the crunch of raw vegetables to cooked ones, especially if they are cut into interesting shapes and called fun names like “broccoli trees,” “carrot coins,” “green pepper pinwheels,” or “celery pick-up sticks.” Serve alongside dips such as hummus, yogurt, or low-fat salad dressing.

ADD FRUITS AND VEGETABLES TO FAVORITE FOODS: Make smoothies with fresh or frozen fruit. Add shredded vegetables to burgers, sandwiches, casseroles, or meatloaf. Add pureed vegetables to sauces. Add fruit to cereal or yogurt. Add sliced vegetables to soups, stews, and pizza. Be creative and let your imagination “go wild!”

PLANT A FRUIT AND VEGETABLE GARDEN: Children are more likely to eat the fruits and vegetables they have planted and nurtured. It’s a wonderful learning experience! Garden produce is less expensive, fresher, and more nutritious and delicious. If you can’t grow a garden, visit a farmer’s market or grow herbs in a container or on a windowsill.

INVOLVE YOUR CHILDREN IN PLANNING SNACKS AND MEALS: The more children contribute and take part in planning, cooking, and preparation of meals and snacks, the more likely they will want to try their creations.

SERVE 100% FRUIT JUICE: Instead of soda and sugary fruit drinks, offer your child 100% fruit juice. For a healthier soda alternative, create fruit juice spritzers: one-third of their favorite 100% fruit juice, two-thirds seltzer.

BE A GOOD ROLE MODEL: Children learn many of their behaviors by observing and imitating what grown-ups and older siblings do. Dine as a family as regularly as possible and let your children observe you eat your fruits and vegetables. Make sure to exhibit a positive attitude about eating the fruits and vegetables.

DO NOT GIVE UP: It can take 6 or more times of trying a new food before children will accept it. Serve the new foods alongside familiar foods. Encourage children to be adventurous with food. When you introduce them to a new food, allow them to sample the food and then decide “no thank you” or “yes please” to more. Not only will children be able to try something new but get to practice good manners too.

Most importantly, make mealtime fun and enjoyable!

ADAPTED FROM:
Blythedale Children’s Hospital *Eat Well, Be Well* nutrition outreach program and FoodPlay Productions, LLC

DISCLAIMER:

Food should be fun for children! But, as parents and caregivers, it is important to be mindful of potential choking hazards and allergies associated with your child eating fruits and vegetables. Consult your child's healthcare provider to learn what to due if either of these situations occur.

YOU CAN HELP PREVENT YOUR CHILD FROM CHOCKING

Food and preparation

- Cook and prepare food to the right shape, size, and texture for your child's development.
- Avoid small, sticky, or hard foods that are hard to chew and swallow.

Meals and snack time

- Have your child sit up while eating (no lying down, crawling, or walking).
- Be very careful about letting your child eat in the car or stroller.
- Keep mealtime calm. Avoid distractions, disruptions, and rushing when eating.

Always

- Pay close attention to what your child puts in his or her mouth.
- Watch your child at all times while he or she is eating.

Potential choking hazards for young children

- **Fruits/Vegetables**
  - Cooked or raw whole corn kernels
  - Uncut cherry or grape tomatoes
  - Pieces of hard raw fruits or vegetables, such as apples or raw carrots
  - Whole pieces of canned fruit
  - Uncut grapes, berries, cherries, or melon balls
  - Uncooked dried fruits or vegetables, such as raisins

♥ **ALWAYS WASH HANDS AND ALL FRUITS AND VEGETABLES** ♥

Source: CDC.gov

Printed in the USA
CPSIA information can be obtained
at www.ICGtesting.com
LVHW060048240923
757182LV00084B/111

9 798987 341612